if found, please return to:

for fun ways to
play, flip to the end!

a note from the creator-
Thank you for hiking with me! All illustrations have been hand-drawn by
a local artist & naturalist of the Adirondacks. Every purchase of this
hiking journal supports not only your adventures, but hers too!

TRAIL

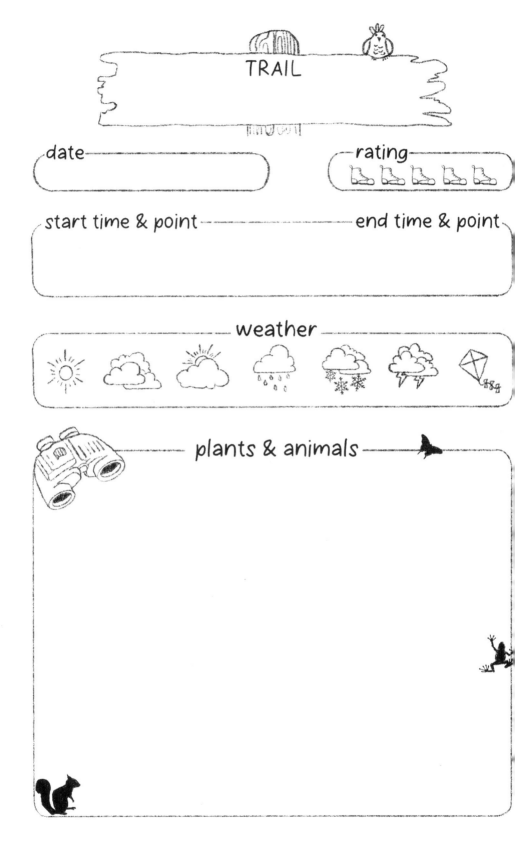

date

rating

start time & point ———— **end time & point**

weather

plants & animals

My favorite part was...

SCAVENGER HUNT

a puddle

hear a
bird song

sign of insects

3 mammals

a tree seed

something
stinky

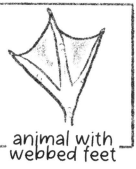

animal with
webbed feet

something
hard

a millipede

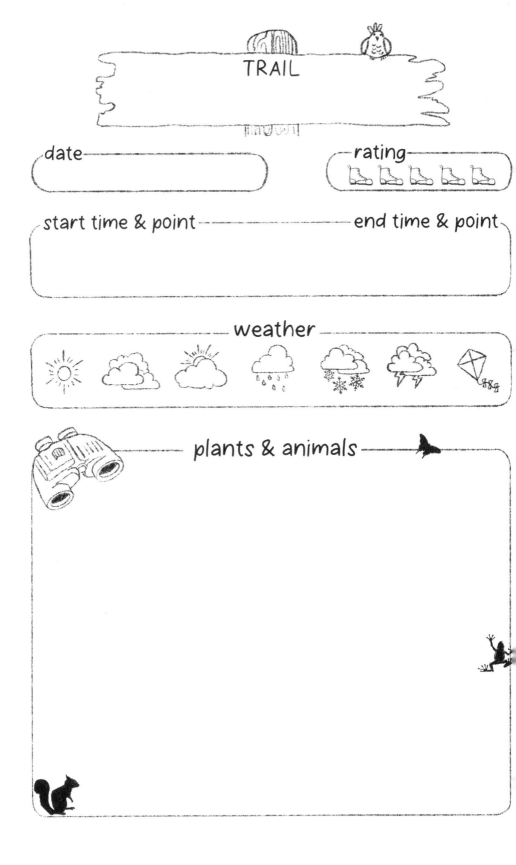

TRAIL

date

rating

start time & point — **end time & point**

weather

plants & animals

My favorite part was...

SCAVENGER HUNT
birds!

big bird

groundbird

seed eater

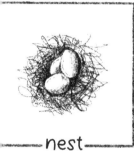
nest

small bird

camouflaged bird

waterbird

colorful bird

insect eater

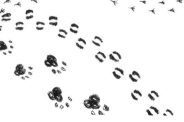

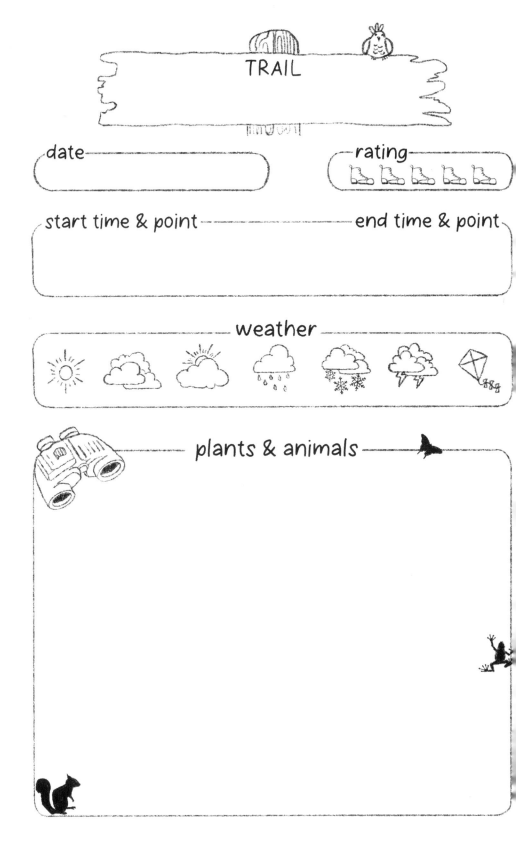

TRAIL

date

rating

start time & point ———— **end time & point**

weather

plants & animals

My favorite part was...

SCAVENGER HUNT
letters!

Bb	Zz	Oo
Aa	Ee	Ww
Tt	Nn	Ll

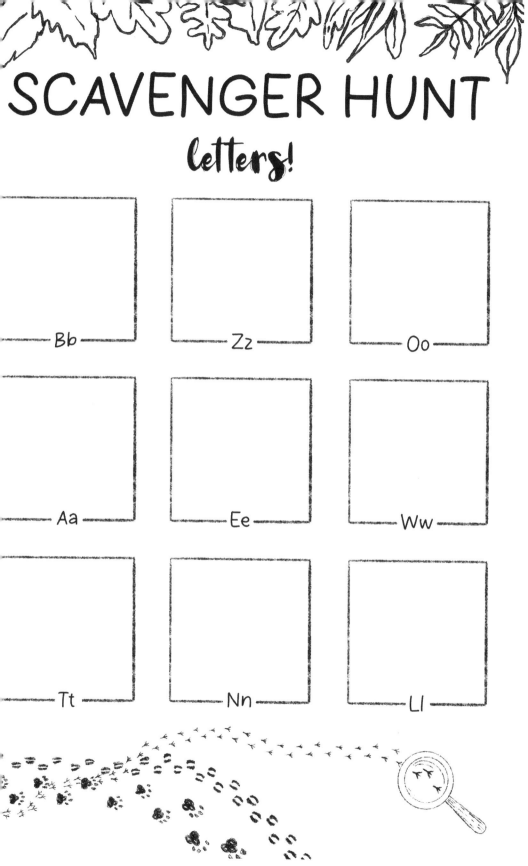

TRAIL

date

rating

start time & point ———— **end time & point**

weather

plants & animals

My favorite part was...

SCAVENGER HUNT
insects!

aquatic insect

beetle

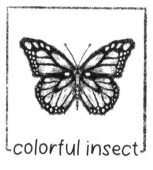
colorful insect

insect eggs

fly

pollinator

hopping insect

shaped like a letter-
you draw!

ant

TRAIL

date

rating

start time & point --- **end time & point**

weather

plants & animals

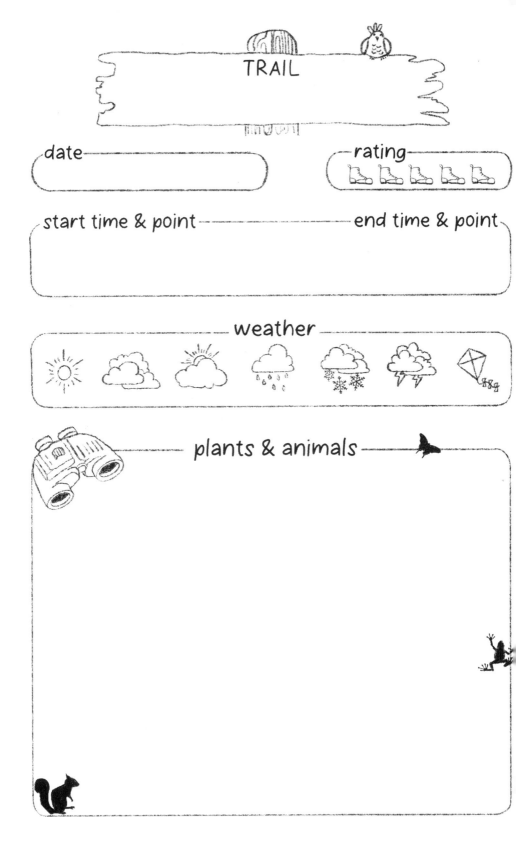

My favorite part was...

SCAVENGER HUNT

something with more than 6 legs

a lichen

a cloud shaped like an animal

a pinecone

something shaped like a V

something sticky

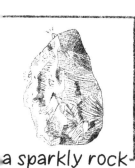

a sparkly rock

a tiny flower

something fun to play with

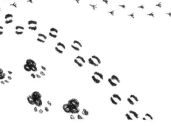

TRAIL

date

rating

start time & point ———————— end time & point

weather

plants & animals

My favorite part was...

SCAVENGER HUNT
colors!

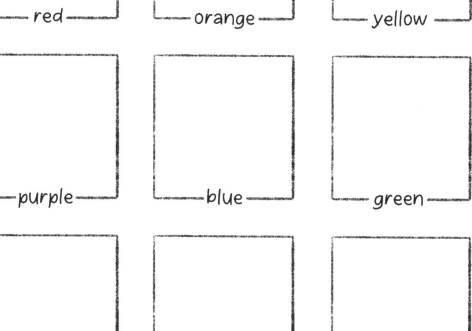

red   orange   yellow

purple   blue   green

white   grey   brown

TRAIL

date

rating

start time & point — end time & point

weather

plants & animals

My favorite part was...

SCAVENGER HUNT
not insects!

spider

snail

?

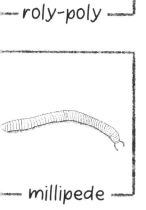

roly-poly

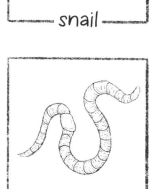

worm

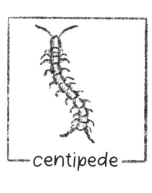

centipede

millipede

shaped like a letter-
you draw!

slug

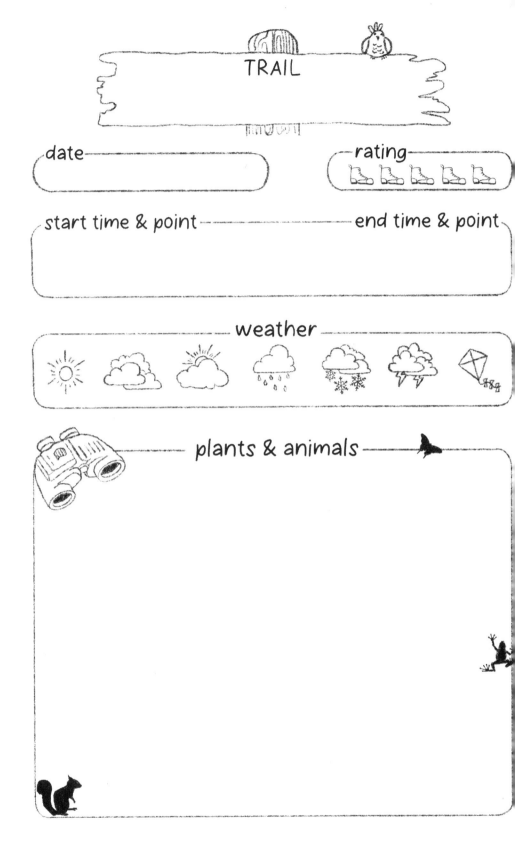

TRAIL

date

rating

start time & point ———————————— **end time & point**

weather

plants & animals

My favorite part was...

SCAVENGER HUNT

a predator

an insect home

4 camouflaged critters

a slow insect

something slippery

something shaped like -J

a log

something heart-shaped

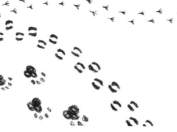
something red

TRAIL

date

rating

start time & point

end time & point

weather

plants & animals

My favorite part was...

SCAVENGER HUNT

gratitude

mom or dad would like	makes a perfect shelter	is your favorite color

is beautiful	makes you smile	can be used as a tool

makes a great camp spot	is fun to watch	you are thankful for

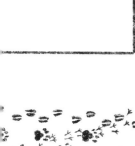

TRAIL

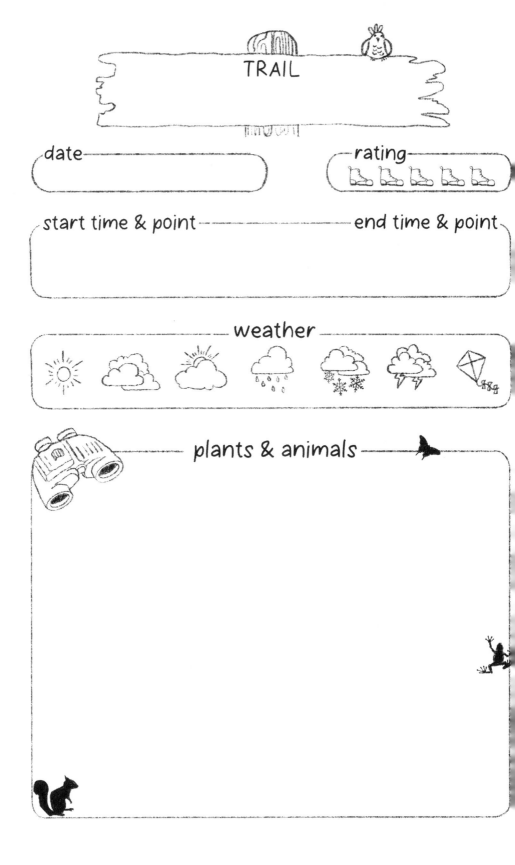

date

rating

start time & point ——————— end time & point

weather

plants & animals

My favorite part was...

SCAVENGER HUNT
leaves!

alternate

opposite

serrate edge

simple

compound

smooth edges

prickly

soft

huge

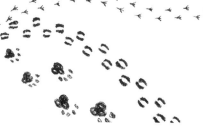

TRAIL

date

rating

start time & point ———————— end time & point

weather

plants & animals

My favorite part was...

SCAVENGER HUNT

opposite leaves

one thing that you love

a scavenger

a tree with peeling bark

something edible

a seed spread by animals

thorns

a flower with many petals

animal tracks

TRAIL

date

rating

start time & point — end time & point

weather

plants & animals

My favorite part was...

SCAVENGER HUNT

5 senses!

hear
a loud bird

something
that
feels soft

something
that
smells good

something
animals
like
to eat

something
that looks
beautiful

find 2 types
of leaves

smell
the earth

listen for
the
sound of water

feel wind
on your face

TRAIL

date

rating

start time & point
end time & point

weather

plants & animals

My favorite part was...

SCAVENGER HUNT
flowers!

a cluster of small flowers

a flowering bush

shaped like a bell

smells good

with 3 petals

with a pollinator

big flower

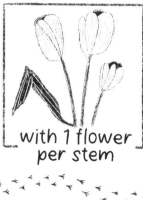
with 1 flower per stem

with 5 petals

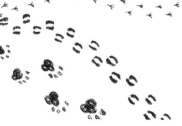

TRAIL

date

rating

start time & point

end time & point

weather

plants & animals

My favorite part was...

SCAVENGER HUNT

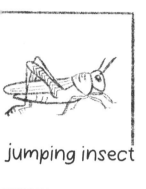

jumping insect

an insectivore

something fascinating

3 bird species

compound leaf

a seed that travels by wind

an animal with scales

shaped like letter -O

something that's your favorite color

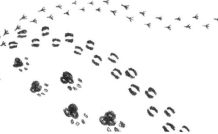

TRAIL

date

rating

start time & point ———— **end time & point**

weather

plants & animals

My favorite part was...

SCAVENGER HUNT

letters!

Aa	Nn	Tt
Ff	Oo	Xx
Pp	Ii	Gg

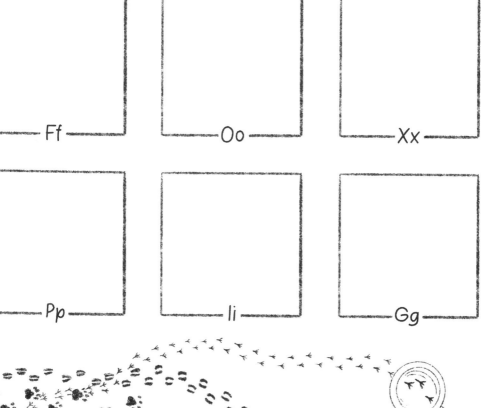

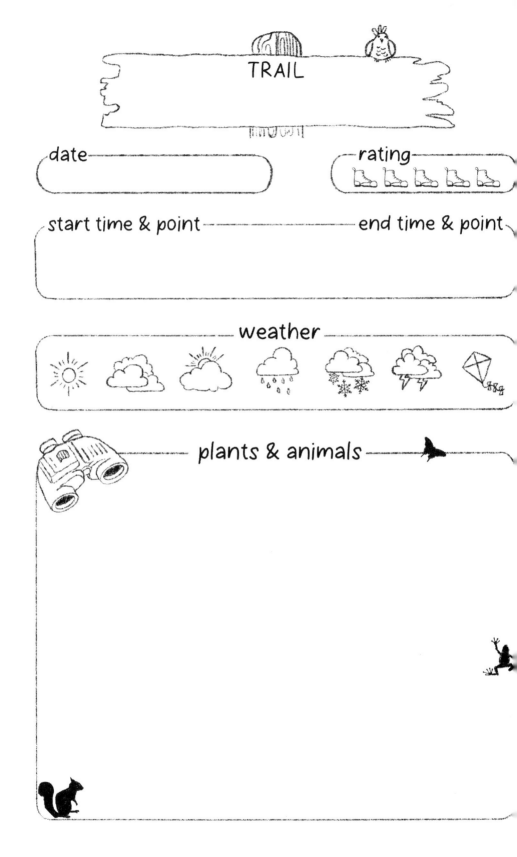

TRAIL

date

rating

start time & point ———— end time & point

weather

plants & animals

My favorite part was...

SCAVENGER HUNT
flower life cycle!

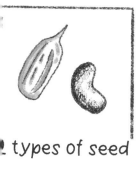
types of seed

cotyledon

a sprout

adult plant

flower

pollinator

fruit

2 types of seed dispersal

water

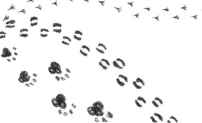

TRAIL

date

rating

start time & point ———— **end time & point**

weather

plants & animals

My favorite part was...

SCAVENGER HUNT

moss

something that starts with -R

something that is fun to climb

2 conifers

a fast insect

a flower

a serrate leaf

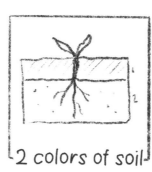
2 colors of soil

animal scat

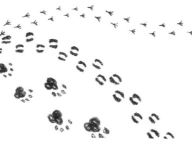

TRAIL

date

rating

start time & point

end time & point

weather

plants & animals

My favorite part was...

SCAVENGER HUNT

let's count!

1 mammal	2 fungi	3 animal homes
4 seeds	5 birds	6 rocks
7 holes	8 insects	9 different leaves

TRAIL

date

rating

start time & point ———— **end time & point**

weather

plants & animals

My favorite part was...

SCAVENGER HUNT
animals!

scat

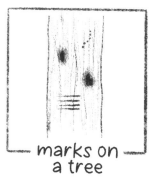

marks on
a tree

a rodent

a burrow

an amphibian

fur

a pet

a feather

with spots

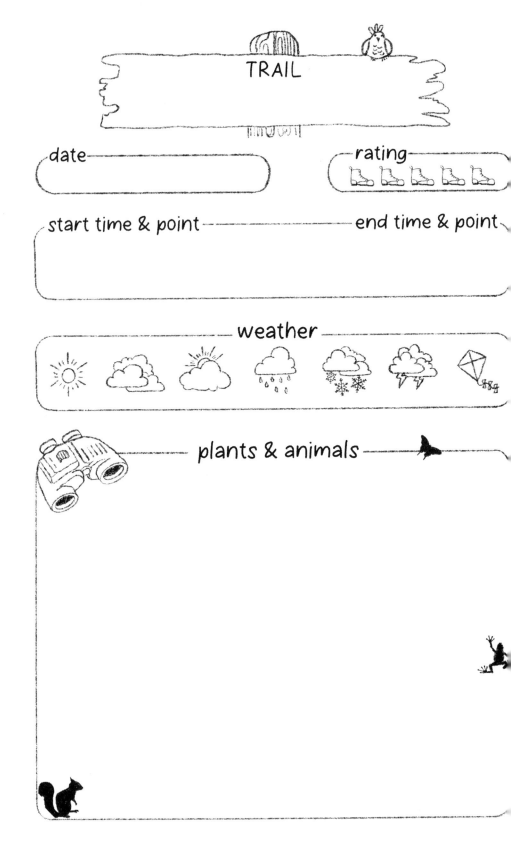

TRAIL

date

rating

start time & point

end time & point

weather

plants & animals

My favorite part was...

SCAVENGER HUNT

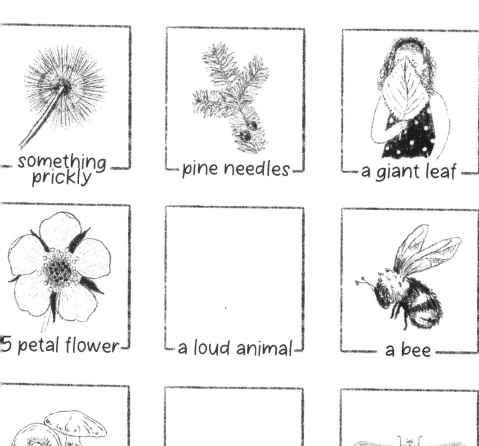

something prickly

pine needles

a giant leaf

5 petal flower

a loud animal

a bee

2 fungi

something white

a flying insect

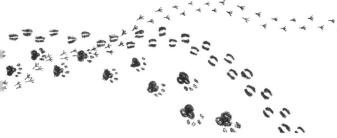

TRAIL

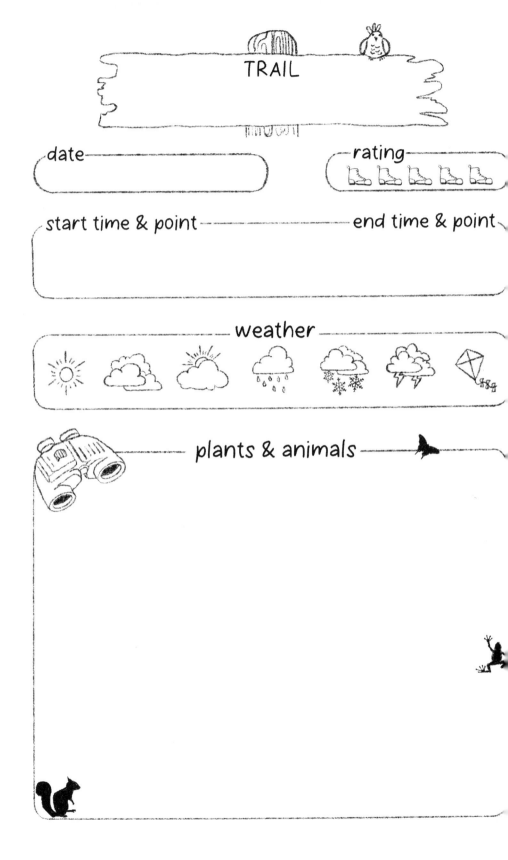

date

rating

start time & point — end time & point

weather

plants & animals

My favorite part was...

SCAVENGER HUNT
textures!

a smooth rock

something soft

a prickly stem

something squishy

a bumpy leaf

something scratchy

something fluffy

a rough rock

3 types of tree bark

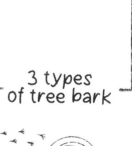

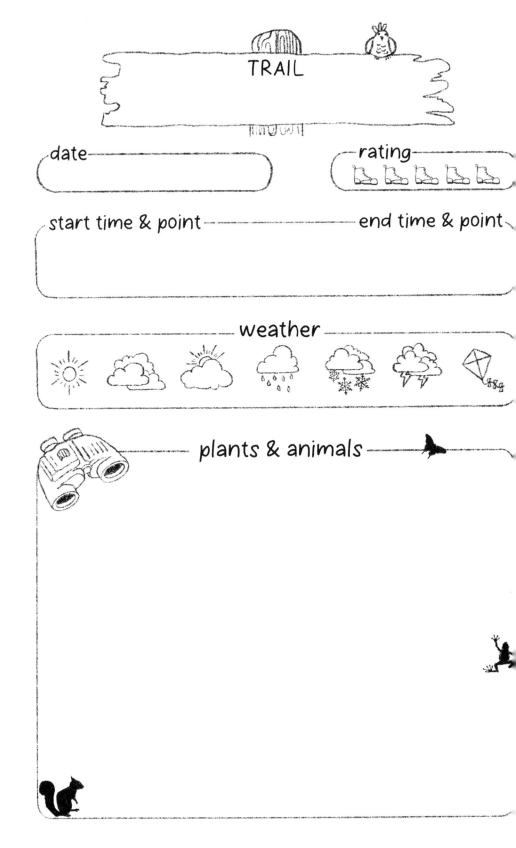

TRAIL

date

rating

start time & point ———————————— **end time & point**

weather

plants & animals

My favorite part was...

SCAVENGER HUNT

a bird eating

a seed pod

5 different leaves

an ant

something I'm thankful for

a flower with an insect

a vine

something that doesn't belong

a nest

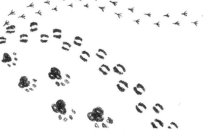

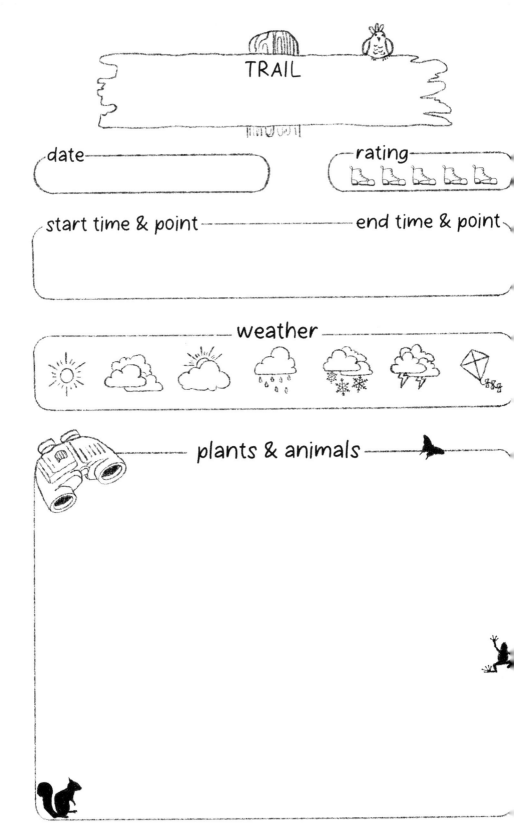

TRAIL

date

rating

start time & point ———— **end time & point**

weather

plants & animals

My favorite part was...

SCAVENGER HUNT
trees

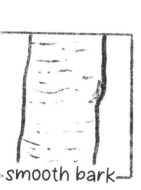
smooth bark

rough bark

sap

pinecone

conifer

deciduous

sapling

wide tree

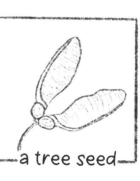
a tree seed

TRAIL

date

rating

start time & point — **end time & point**

weather

plants & animals

My favorite part was...

SCAVENGER HUNT

a bird eating

a seed pod

5 different leaves

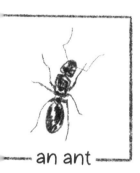
an ant

something I'm thankful for

a flower with an insect

a vine

something that doesn't belong

a nest

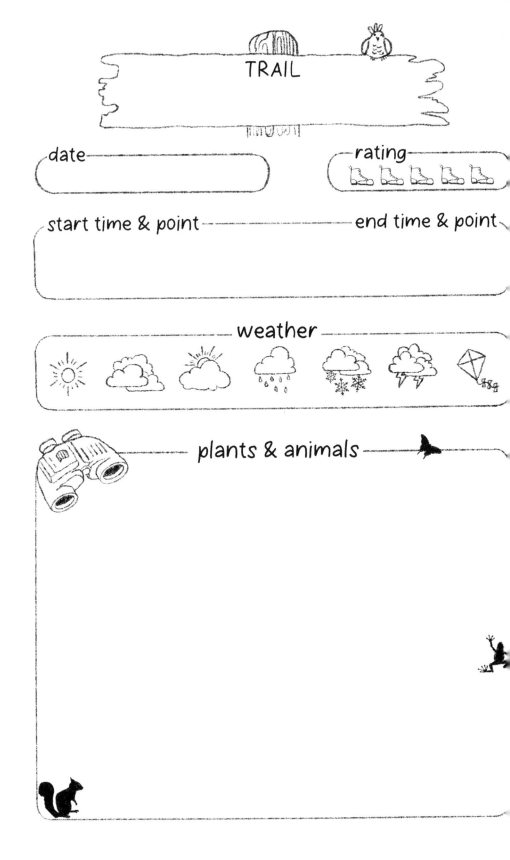

TRAIL

date

rating

start time & point ———— **end time & point**

weather

plants & animals

My favorite part was...

SCAVENGER HUNT

seeds!

travels by wind

seed case

prickly seed

pod

berry

pinecone

floating seed

hidden under leaf

nut

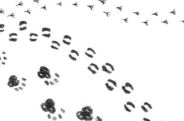

TRAIL

date

rating

start time & point ———— **end time & point**

weather

plants & animals

My favorite part was...

SCAVENGER HUNT

smooth bark

something fluffy

a beetle

a bird in a tree

a spider web

a pollinator

3 seeds

an animal with a shell

starts with -S

TRAIL

date

rating

start time & point ———————————— end time & point

weather

plants & animals

My favorite part was...

SCAVENGER HUNT
you create!

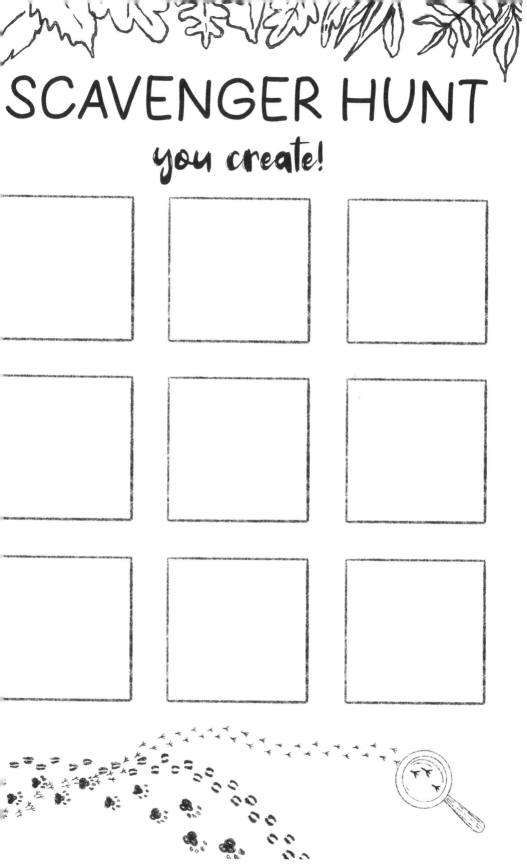

some fun ways to play:

BINGO! find 3 in a row
OR
find as many as you can

color in the square
when you find it
OR
mark an X in the square
when you find it

*when the square is
empty, you draw what
you find!

*letters: can start with or be in
the shape of that letter

Made in the USA
Coppell, TX
16 November 2024

40394520R00065